HEMINGWAY IN 90 MINUTES

HEMINGWAY IN 90 MINUTES. Copyright © 2005 by Paul
Strathern. All rights reserved, including the right to reproduce
this book or portions thereof in any form. For information,
address: Ivan R. Dee, Publisher, 1332 North Halsted Street,
Chicago 60622. Manufactured in the United States of America
and printed on acid-free paper.

www.ivanrdee.com

Library of Congress Cataloging-in-Publication Data:
Strathern, Paul, 1940–
    Hemingway in 90 minutes / Paul Strathern.
        p. cm.
    Includes bibliographical references and index.
    ISBN 1-56663-659-0 (cloth : alk. paper) —
    ISBN 1-56663-658-2 (pbk. : alk. paper)
    1. Hemingway, Ernest, 1899–1961. 2. Authors, American—
20th century—Biography. 3. Journalists—United States—
Biography. I. Title: Hemingway in ninety minutes. II. Title.
PS3515.E37Z8825 2005
813'.52—dc22
                                    2005007511

Contents

HEMINGWAY IN 90 MINUTES

Introduction

At the age of eighteen, Ernest Hemingway was serving as an ambulance driver with the Red Cross in northern Italy during the First World War. In the summer of 1918 the Austrians launched an assault in an attempt to cross the River Piave, north of Venice, and the Italians dug in on the western bank resisting heavy artillery barrages. The Red Cross put in a request for volunteers to run the canteens in the villages behind the front lines. Hemingway volunteered and was posted to the beleagured village of Fossalta di Piave, close by the river.

The night of July 8 was hot and moonless. Under cover of darkness, Hemingway set off on his bicycle to deliver packs of cigarettes, bars of chocolate, and the latest batch of postcards from home to the men in the frontline trenches. He parked his bike behind the wall of the command post, pulled his helmet on tight, ducked, and ran forward across the open ground to the trench. This was not the first of Hemingway's deliveries to the front line, and the Italians were glad to see him. His crude Yankee attempts at Italian made them laugh.

Just after midnight the Austrians fired a mortar shell filled with shrapnel toward the Italian trenches. Hemingway and the Italians tensed as they heard the telltale cough of the mortar firing, followed by the ominous chugging sound of the canister hurtling on its long arc up into the night sky above no-man's-land, and then its descent. The canister would explode on impact. In Hemingway's own words:

> . . . there was a flash, as when a blast-furnace door is swung open, and a roar that started white and went red and on and on in a rushing wind. . . . The ground was torn up and in

8

front of my head there was a splintered beam of wood. In the jolt of my head I heard somebody crying. I thought somebody was screaming.

When he came to, Hemingway crawled toward one of the badly wounded Italians. Hemingway managed to get to his feet despite being splattered with pieces of shrapnel in both legs, and hauled the wounded Italian over his shoulder in a fireman's lift. He then began lugging him 150 yards back toward the command post. But after he had crossed just 50 yards he was caught by a burst of machine-gun fire, which hit him in the right knee and foot:

The machine-gun bullet just felt like a sharp smack on my leg with an icy snow ball. However it spilled me. But I got up again and got my wounded into the dugout. I kind of collapsed at the dugout.

He could remember nothing between having been hit by the machine-gun fire and collapsing at the end of his staggering journey. He reckoned he must have been acting on instinct alone. The Italians in the command post were convinced he was going to die. His torn uniform was drenched in blood from the man he had been carrying, and they thought Hemingway had been shot through the chest. In the end they got him onto a stretcher and laid him out in a roofless shed alongside some wounded and dying Italian soldiers. Above him in the night sky he could see the faint light of stars and the fireworks of the exploding artillery shells. He began praying, convinced he was about to die.

Hemingway was later awarded the Italian Silver Medal of Military Valor. His citation described how he:

> gave proof of courage and self-sacrifice. Gravely wounded by numerous pieces of shrapnel from an enemy shell, with an admirable spirit of brotherhood, before taking care of himself, he rendered generous assistance to the Italian soldiers more seriously wounded by the same explosion and did not

allow himself to be carried elsewhere until they had been evacuated.

Severe doubts have been cast on the second part of Hemingway's exploit. With both legs embedded with shrapnel, how could he possibly have carried a wounded Italian soldier across that 150 yards, let alone the last 100 yards when he had been hit in the leg by machine-gun fire? But the citation to his award, presumably relying upon the testimony of an officer who was present, undeniably speaks of "generous assistance" and suggests selfless valor.

It has been suggested that Hemingway did not in fact have his leg shot away from beneath him by machine-gun fire, that this part of the story is sheer embelishment. On the other hand, there would have been machine-gun fire, and his staggering movements could well have shifted the fresh shrapnel in his leg, making it feel like that "icy snow ball" he felt hit his right knee. We will never know the truth for certain. Yet the evidence, and his subsequent character, indicates that Hemingway was certainly capable of bravery. Unfortunately he was also a colossal fibber. A simple act of bravery was never enough. His actions always had to be bigger and better than anyone else's. It is hardly surprising that eventually people began to doubt *everything* he ever claimed.

Soon after arriving at the hospital at Milan, Hemingway wrote home "so that you hear from me first rather than the newspapers." He specifically mentions an x-ray revealing a bullet in his knee, including sufficient medical detail to suggest this claim was true. But other claims are less credible, such as his unnecessary announcement that "I'm the first American wounded in Italy." (Not true, and he knew it.) In a second letter he speaks of "the 227 wounds I got from the trench mortar" (another unnecessary mythical exactitude). He is filled with jovial bravado, telling the folks back home, "The Italian surgeon did a peach of a job on my right knee joint and right foot. Took 28 stitches and assures me that I will be able to walk as well as ever."

What he does not mention is bravery of an ostensibly less heroic sort. To fend off night terrors when he was afraid his leg might have to be amputated, he took to knocking himself out with brandy. At one stage he also visited a ward for men who had suffered serious genital wounds, suggesting that he may have suffered a similar wound and been worried about its effect on his virility.

But by the time he emerged from the hospital he was determined to put his worries behind him. He had a smart British officer–style replacement uniform made by a fashionable Milan tailor, but he refused to appear in public until this was sewn with his wound stripes and medal ribbon. Despite being able to walk only on crutches, he had a deep irrational fear of being mistaken for a malingerer. A studio photo for which he posed at this time shows his uniform complete with U.S. military insignia (to which he was not entitled) and no sign of Red Cross insignia.

By December 1918 he was able to limp, with the aid of a stick, to the Officers' Club in Milan. (As a member of the Red Cross he was by custom accredited with the rank of lieutenant.)

Here he learned of the armistice signed between Italy and Austria, and celebrated with a British major called Dorman-Smith, who had been in the war since 1914 and had collected several medals for bravery. These medals were evidently a little too much for Hemingway, and Dorman-Smith left under the impression that "this harmless-looking Red Cross youngster had been badly wounded leading Arditi storm troops on Monte Grappa."

Less than two months later, Hemingway sailed back across the Atlantic for New York, aboard the liner SS *Giuseppe Verdi*. By now he was every inch a hero—complete with shiny, knee-length military boots, a well-cut black Italian military cloak with a silver clasp, and a distinguished cane for his limp. The first reporter aboard, from the *New York Star*, quickly spotted the dashing hero, and pestered him for an interview. America needed heroes, and the *Star*'s reporter gleefully obliged, making claims far beyond any evidence that even Hemingway could have supplied. His article described Hemingway's body as having "more scars than any

14

other man, in or out of uniform, who defied the shrapnel of the Central Powers."

In his own small way, Hemingway *had* been a hero, but this was not enough—either for the American public or for Hemingway. The arrival of the limping hero, with his medal and black military cloak, in suburban Oak Park, Chicago, caused a sensation. Invited to speak at the high school he had left just two years earlier, he addressed a packed auditorium. Here he recounted how, after being wounded at Fossalta, he had volunteered for service as an officer with the crack Italian Arditti and seen action in the mountain war. Afterward he was interviewed for the school magazine. In reply to the admiring cub reporter's questions, he elaborated on how he had fought with the Arditti in three major battles— on the Piave front, at Monte Grappa, and at Vittorio Veneto. In this collaboration between the high school cub reporter and the noncombatant Red Cross volunteer, a myth of truly heroic porportions at last began to take on a life of its own.

Hemingway was always willing to go along with this myth, and actually encouraged it—at least in public. To himself, he was more ambivalent. Certainly the Hemingway who became a great writer initially had his reservations. He wished to convey the clear truth of his exploits, without exaggeration. And he was not afraid to hint at more damaging truths. He chose to make the autobiographical hero of his first serious novel, *The Sun Also Rises*, sexually impotent, just as he may temporarily have become as a result of his shrapnel wounds. The hero of his next novel, *A Farewell to Arms*, which recounts his experiences as a Red Cross volunteer on the northern Italian front, tells a distinctly modest version of the incident in which he was wounded and for which he received a medal. But no one seemed to notice. By this stage the Hemingway myth was already beginning to obscure the lucid honesty of the writer.

Hemingway's Life and Works

Ernest Hemingway was born in Oak Park, a prosperous suburb of Chicago, on July 21, 1899. His father, Ed Hemingway, was a tall, broad-shouldered man with a thick black beard who loved hunting. He was a doctor by profession but made money in the Chicago real estate boom. This enabled him to buy a remote farm in the Michigan woods, where he could hunt to his heart's content.

When Hemingway was just seven weeks old he was shipped from Oak Park to the family's holiday home in the backwoods—a journey involving a 250-mile steamer trip up Lake Michigan and a ride on a narrow-gauge railway through the forest, ending in a row across the lake to the homestead. Throughout his childhood, Ernest was indoctrinated by his father in the ways of the backwoods—how to fish, how to chop wood with an axe, how to hunt deer, how to shoot game. The rules of the wild were strict. Nothing was to be killed for killing's sake: anything you killed you had to eat. Young Ernest learned his first lesson by having to eat the tough, malodorous meat of a porcupine he had shot for fun.

Ernest's mother, Grace Hemingway, had been destined for a career as an opera singer, but this was curtailed because of her weak eyesight. On her debut at Madison Square Garden, she was all but blinded by the glare of the footlights, which gave her an incapacitating headache. She returned to Chicago where she became a music teacher, and finally married Ed. She continued to teach music after her marriage, one consequence of which was that Ed cooked all the family meals.

With hindsight it is clear that young Ernest would have enjoyed (and benefited from) the presence of a young brother, but this would not occur until it was too late and Ernest was almost grown up. Ernest's early years were spent in a household of sisters. Such circumstances often serve as a great bolster to the male ego: the child becomes the center of female attention, dressed up and looked after by doting sisters. But Ernest's mother did her best to check this. As a result, the young man developed a grudge against his mother, considering her interfering and manipulative. By his early twenties he was telling his friends that he "hated" his mother, referring to her as "that bitch." In fact, during his earliest years he seems to have been very close to his mother, becoming her favorite. Among other things, she dressed baby Ernest in girl's clothing for his first few years. The effect on his playmates was predictable. As a result, young Ernest seems to have felt the need to assert his manhood forcefully from an early age—in the process developing a pugnacious side to his character.

Another trait that Ernest developed at an early age was fibbing. Initially this was a natural reaction to his father's overstrict rules of conduct in the wild. Everything had to be learned the proper way (invariably the hard, painstaking way), and from then on it had to be performed just right. Young Ernest was eager to shine, but instead he mainly felt bullied. Returning home after expeditions with his father, he began telling his sisters exaggerated yarns about his exploits. As early as the age of four he boasted to his grandfather that he had managed to stop a running horse single-handed. His grandfather, an astute businessman, reckoned the young boy's imagination would either make him famous or land him in jail.

At school, Ernest quickly asserted his presence in sports. He was big and tough, and was soon on the swimming, track, and boxing teams. He also found a place on the football squad, but despite his powerful physique he did not fulfill his potential there. Hemingway was never much of a team player—unless, of course, he was in charge. Although undeniably intelligent, he showed little interest in developing academic skills, preferring to maintain a hearty anti-intellectual attitude. Nonetheless he showed exceptional skill at

English—writing pieces for the school magazine that showed a precocious skill in describing physical action. Particularly noticeable was his meticulous attention to detail: here at last was a skill, intimately connected to the life of action he so loved, which he did not have to learn from his father. This was his own skill, his very own form of expression, which he could learn in his own way, and in which he could attempt to express how he really felt.

All this appeared very healthy and normal, but there seems to have been a faint edge of psychological disturbance to his character even at this age. At home the family was not all that it seemed. Big tough Ed Hemingway suffered increasingly from bouts of black depression. Meanwhile sentimental Grace Hemingway developed a somewhat excessive affection for one of her good-looking female pupils. Taking along two of her children, she would occasionally leave and spend the weekend at her pupil's house, a habit that led to local gossip about lesbianism.

Ernest had difficulty with his love, and hate, for his mother, which was echoed in his intense yet ambivalent feelings for his father. Initially Ernest had hero-worshiped Ed, though this had later been counterbalanced by a natural rebelliousness. But his father's depressions resulted in Ed succumbing more and more to Grace's will. Ernest watched in horror as his hero became a defeated man. By the age of seventeen he still felt intensely close to both his parents, even loved them, yet couldn't restrain his deepening feelings of contempt for them. This undertow of contradictory emotions in Hemingway meant that beneath the tough-guy exterior a distincly complex and contradictory character was developing. Evidence of this disturbance was becoming more evident in what appeared at the time to be merely normal teenage foibles such as fibbing, exaggeration, and self-mythologizing. Hemingway would never outgrow these essentially childish traits.

But young Ernest was big enough to carry off, or at least defend, most of his boasts. His fellow pupils learned not to question his claims: Ernest's need to believe such boasts seemed to be unnaturally strong. It was already becoming part of a carapace that protected a clear-eyed sensitivity, developing separately of its own accord. The innocent eye was becoming detached from the tough guy who seemed so necessary to protect it.

With the outbreak of the First World War in Europe, President Woodrow Wilson declared his determination to keep America out of the war and maintain a policy of "peace at any price." Yet many young Americans were determined to get involved. Some, such as the young Southern would-be writer William Faulkner, traveled north to Canada to join the British Flying Corps. Others volunteered for noncombatant duties in ambulance units. At first Hemingway showed little interest in the war, which attracted only minor attention in suburban Oak Park. Even after America finally entered the war in April 1917, Hemingway seems to have taken no more than a normal patriotic interest.

That year, at age seventeen, Ernest graduated from high school. He had no intention of becoming a doctor, as his father had hoped. Instead he took a job as a junior reporter on the *Kansas*

City Star, then regarded as one of the country's leading newspapers. Kansas City was one of the rough and ready, prosperous new cities of the Midwest, equally renowned for its jazz and its whores. (The main street in the red-light district was nicknamed "Woodrow Wilson Avenue" because there you could get "a piece at any price.") But it remained something of its pioneer innocence. Its values were those of an energetic, optimistic America which believed that a man could achieve anything if he set his mind to it and worked hard. He could be stymied only by his own character flaws. Hemingway thrived in this atmosphere, and his editors were soon beating his style into shape. Articles had to be brief, clear, and to the point: he soon got the message. There was only one complaint about the eager new reporter: when sent on a story, he was liable to become distracted by what he regarded as a better story. Sent to cover a story in a hospital, he would end up riding off in an ambulance in pursuit of a sensational accident. According to a former colleague, "He seemed always to want to be where the action was."

In the dance halls of Kansas City, filled with farm hands on a binge, and increasingly by soldiers going off to war, there were frequent fights. Inevitably Hemingway soon decided that he wanted to go to war too. But his attempts to enlist were rejected. He had poor sight in one eye, a legacy inherited from his mother. Characteristically, he claimed that this resulted from a boxing match, in which a dirty opponent had "thumbed" his eye. Late in 1917, he ran into someone who told him that the Red Cross was accepting volunteers. Hemingway offered, was accepted, and after a brief training period was shipped across the Atlantic. He ended up in northern Italy where he was employed as an ambulance driver, and quickly volunteered for duties closer to the front line. Three weeks later he was seriously wounded when the mortar shell landed near him in the trench, and was shipped back to the Red Cross hospital in Milan.

The newly established Ospedale Croce Rossa Americana had eighteen nurses and just four patients. Perhaps inevitably, the eighteen-year-old wounded hero soon fell in love with one of the nurses who looked after him on the night shift. This was Agnes von Kurowsky, a tall, dark-haired volunteer who had been brought up in Washington, D.C. Their attraction was mutual, though they reacted in different ways. Hemingway was essentially a sexual innocent, despite his boasts to his schoolfriends and young fellow reporters in Kansas City. He found himself smitten by the full force of teenage love. Agnes, on the other hand, was almost thirty and wary of a deep involvement which she felt sure could not last. They kissed, but she would not allow things to go further, telling him that she must remain "professional" in her work. When Hemingway was sufficiently recovered to leave the hospital, and had outfitted himself in his smart new uniform, they made up a party with some of the other nurses and their American soldier friends and went to the races at San Sciro. Hemingway would remember this as an idyllic day, every detail of the track and the autumnal weather etched with utmost clarity in his memory. When Agnes was later transferred to Florence, 170 miles to the south, they wrote to each other every day.

Although Hemingway liked to play the hero in public, his private thoughts on this subject did not include such an element of show. He may have felt the need to fool others, but he wasn't about to fool himself. At the front, before being wounded, he had encountered a grey-haired fifty-year-old Italian soldier, and joked to him in his pidgin Italian: "You're *troppo vecchio* [too old] for this war, *papa*." But the old man had replied seriously, "I can die as well as any man." Hemingway had been deeply struck by this remark, which took on a new significance after his own brush with death. Later, when he encountered Major Dorman-Smith in the Milan Officers' Club, he was particularly struck by the Britisher's laconic modesty about his bravery. This, Hemingway felt, was how a genuine hero should behave: with reticent, understated grace. This was how he too would now conduct himself in public—to begin with, at any rate, until he was "coaxed" into telling his story. But less superficially, he was inspired by Dorman-Smith's attitude toward death, which the British officer modestly illustrated by quoting from

Shakespeare: "I care not; a man can die but once; we owe God a death." This was how a hero faced death. Just like the fifty-year-old Italian soldier, Dorman-Smith did not ignore death: he faced up to it. Inside Hemingway, the public boaster was a young man who was forming his own ideas about heroism. At the same time, the very idea of death became a kind of talisman. He was developing an undeniably morbid streak, though at the time he had no idea how much this was a matter of psychological inheritance. (As we shall see, the three immediate generations of Hemingway's family would be blighted by suicides.)

Then the war was over, and it was time to go home. He and Agnes promised to write to each other. The arrival of the public hero back in Oak Park, in his flamboyant Italian cloak, soon began to pall. He seemed to want just to sit around the house all day, with no intention of taking on anything so unheroic as a job. The letters from Agnes became less frequent; then she told him that she had fallen in love with an Italian officer from Naples. Hemingway would later describe how he "cauterized" his feelings for her by embarking upon a binge of "booze and other women." The truth was rather more mundane, if nonetheless painful. He retired to bed with a severe bout of hypochondria, then dashed off an angry letter to one of Agnes's nursing colleagues in Italy. In it he expressed the vehement hope that when Agnes returned and stepped off the gangplank at New York she would fall flat on her face and smash all her front teeth. It took time, but gradually he got over the hurt to his pride and public image. His private feelings were another matter: they lay in his memory, their immediacy undimmed, their fineness untainted by acrimony. Eight years later, Agnes would reappear as one of his most deeply felt female creations.

After a certain amount of friction, Ernest's family encouraged him to move out. He decided to try his luck across the border in Toronto, where his credentials as a former reporter on the *Kansas City Star* were good enough to get him a job writing pieces for the weekly magazine section of the *Toronto Star*. In between times he began producing short stories. Contrary to his parents' opinion, he had not been simply loafing about the house—he had in fact begun writing. At first he tried recounting experiences from the war; later he turned to telling anecdotes from his days as a reporter in Kansas City; then he began really enjoying himself by writing stories about his hunting, fishing, and shooting trips in Michigan. He sent his stories to magazines, but no one was interested.

Eventually he returned to Chicago, where he took a cheap room. He still sent occasional stories to the *Toronto Star*, and managed to supplement this income by going a few rounds at the boxing gyms as a professional sparring partner. This was a hard, brave, and dangerous way for a middle-class young man to earn a few bucks, but it didn't last long. Nonetheless it quickly gained its permanent place in the Hemingway hall of mythology as he established himself in his own way among the young bohemian crowd in Chicago.

"Hem," as he liked to be known, was soon a leading figure at the parties given by penniless young artists and writers. At one of these he met

Elizabeth Hadley Richardson, who had recently arrived in Chicago from St. Louis and was recovering from the depressing task of looking afer her dying mother. Hadley was attractive, had inherited a small private income, and was eight years older than Hemingway. As with Agnes, the age difference seemed to have an effect on him, and he soon fell in love with her. For her part, she was bowled over by the attentions of this apparently larger-than-life figure—who seemed to be around her age, a misunderstanding that Hemingway did nothing to discourage. Hadley had lived a sheltered life, and responded to Hemingway's tales of wartime heroism with wide-eyed admiration. Europe was the place to be, he assured her, that was where they knew how to live properly. It was a whirlwind romance, and they were soon engaged. They would marry and then go to live in Italy. Hemingway had no money, but both of them could easily live on Hadley's income in cheaper Europe.

Another important influence on Hemingway's life at this time was the writer Sherwood Anderson, who had just returned from Paris.

The forty-four-year-old Anderson was already an established writer and had just published his finest work, *Winesburg, Ohio*. It contained twenty-three thematically linked stories conveying the "lives of quiet desperation" lived by the inhabitants on all levels of society in a small Midwestern town. Particularly striking was Anderson's ability to convey how the life of apparently simple ordinary people could be as rich and subtle as that of more privileged and sophisticated citizens.

Anderson became Hemingway's mentor, advising him on what books to read so that he could make up for his lack of a college education. Hemingway also learned from Anderson's style, particularly his combination of everyday speech and sparse, unvarnished description. When Hemingway told Anderson that he planned to go to Italy after he was married, Anderson advised him to go to Paris instead. That was the artistic capital of the world, where a young writer could be taken seriously and learn of the latest literary developments as well as mixing with the coming generation of writers.

Hemingway and Hadley were married in March 1921 and set off across the Atlantic for Paris, carrying a number of letters of recommendation from Sherwood Anderson to various well-known figures. These included Gertrude Stein, the leading American avant-garde writer in Paris; Sylvia Beach, the American owner of the celebrated bookshop and meeting place Shakespeare and Company, who would become James Joyce's publisher; and the poet and literary publicist Ezra Pound.

Years later Hemingway would romanticize his first years in Paris with Hadley, telling of "how Paris was in the early days when we were very poor and very happy." As always with Hemingway's stories, this had its grain of truth. He and Hadley were indeed happy together, but they were far from poor, certainly compared with some of the exiled writers who were struggling to make ends meet in the Latin Quarter. As ever, Hemingway was determined to be different: he wasn't about to be just another American in Paris. To save money he insisted that he and Hadley take a cheap two-room apartment in a rough working-class neighborhood. The only source of heat in the place was a small coal-burning fire, and as they lived on the fourth floor, Hemingway had to lug the sacks of coal up several flights of stairs. According to Hemingway, "Hunger was good discipline." He explained how:

> You got very hungry when you did not eat enough in Paris because all the bakery shops had such good things in the windows and people ate outside on the sidewalk so you saw and smelled the food. . . . You could always go into the Luxembourg Museum and all the paintings were sharpened and clearer and more beautiful if you were belly-empty, hollow-hungry.

It comes as something of a surprise to notice from the photographs of this period that these were the years when Hemingway began to put on weight.

All this "poverty" was quite unnecessary as Hadley had savings and an income of three thousand dollars a year, on top of which Hemingway had arranged to send a regular newsletter from Europe to the *Toronto Star* which would bring in another fifteen hundred dollars a year. At the time, an entire French working-class family was living on the equivalent of around twelve hundred dollars a year. But Hemingway wanted to appear poor, and he also wanted to use the saved money to travel around Europe. He earned further money by giving boxing lessons to fellow Americans. As Hemingway always wanted to win in the ring, these "lessons" usually ended up with his lightweight opponent suffering from a bloodied nose and black eyes. Only the distinctly unathletic Ezra Pound seems to have lasted the pace—but there were reasons for this.

Pound was a difficult man who had his own problems with maintaining his sanity, and Hemingway took an instant dislike to his quirky pretentiousness. One day Pound invited Hemingway around for tea at his small apartment, and Hemingway took particular exception to the oriental knickknacks with which Pound had decorated his home. When Hemingway got back to his own, suitably unpretentious apartment, he sat down and wrote a vicious satirical sketch based on Pound. But to his surprise, none of the little magazines in Paris would accept the piece. Then he discovered why. Pound was an exceptionally generous character: when he discovered someone who was genuinely talented, he did all he could to help that person and promote his or her work. He also gave exceptionally perceptive literary advice. Amazingly, he had already convinced the well-known Irish poet W. B. Yeats to effect a complete transformation of his style (now recognized as a major turning point in Yeats's poetry). On top of this, he had also "discovered" T. S. Eliot and James Joyce. Pound was a force to be reckoned with. Hemingway tore up his satirical piece and decided to go easy on the boxing lessons with Pound. He even invited Pound to look at some of his own stories and poems. Pound's perceptive stylistic criticism hit home, and Hemingway began to write poems in Pound's free-verse, "imagistic" style. Another influence on Hemingway at this time was the formidable Gertrude Stein, whose plain, repetitive "Cubist" style was introducing a new concrete simplicity into the language: "A rose is a rose is a rose is a rose."

Despite their so-called poverty, Hemingway and Hadley managed to get away for frequent holidays. These included an abortive trip to Italy, where Hemingway found it all but impossible to retrace his wartime exploits. Things had changed. He also discovered Spain, where Hemingway quickly found himself enchanted by the spectacle of bullfighting. Here was violence and death enacted in an all but timeless formalized setting. Hemingway continued to ponder on the interaction between nobility and death. Where others might have articulated this in some kind of philosophy, Hemingway preferred to think at a more visceral level. What mattered in the hero was not the power of his intellect but his emotional response. If a man didn't have guts, didn't develop that all but indefinable nobility of being, he would fall prey to inner flaws such as cowardice.

Hemingway's reporting for the *Toronto Star* took him on frequent (expense-paid) trips all over Europe, from Istanbul to Lausanne to Rome. He met the young fascist leader Benito Mussolini, who had just come to power. Hemingway was quick to spot a fellow braggart and dubbed Mussolini "the biggest bluff in Europe." His article on Mussolini is an excellent corrective to all those who consider Hemingway to be lacking in a genuine sense of humor and incapable of deft wit:

> Get hold of a good photo of Signor Mussolini some time and study it. You will see the weakness in his mouth which forces him to scowl the famous Mussolini scowl that is imitated by every 19 year old Fascisto in Italy. . . . And then look at his black shirt and his white spats. There is something wrong, even histrionically, with a man who wears white spats with a black shirt.

The twenty-three-year-old Hemingway's journalistic and literary judgment was both exceptionally informed and exceptionally perceptive. Yet the trouble was, he always had to know more than anyone else about everything. Café conversations with fellow writers often degenerated into pugnacious arguments—followed by a challenge to a boxing match to settle the matter. Even if he won in the ring, this didn't mean that his opinion on Dante was correct—but this didn't seem to occur to him.

Still, Hemingway's private judgments remained astute. He was learning how to write, honing his choices about what to include and what to discard. What should be stated and what should be merely implied? What unspoken knowledge, which the reader gathers for himself, can inform a short story so that it resonates far beyond its few words? Once again he found himself evoking the countryside he had known since childhood, this time in a short story entitled "Up in Michigan":

A steep sandy road ran down the hill to the bay through the timber. From Smith's back door you could look out across the woods that ran down to the lake across the bay. It was very beautiful in the spring and summer, the bay blue and bright and usually white-caps on the lake out beyond the point from the breeze blowing from Charlevoix and Lake Michigan. From Smith's back door Liz could see ore barges way out in the lake going toward Boyne City.

Having absorbed various formative influences, Hemingway was now beginning to develop a distinct style of his own, one that was in accord with his personal view of the world—his private ethos, as distinct from the exaggerated persona that he presented. The deceptive simplicity of this style made it appear almost artless, though in fact it consisted of a highly formal mannerism.

A few of Hemingway's stories now began appearing in the little literary magazines of Paris. Then, with the help of Pound, he published a small, limited edition entitled *Three Stories and Ten Poems*. This included "Up in Michigan" and a number of imagist poems, including one where he evokes his typewriter.

The mills of the gods grind slowly;
But this mill

Chatters in mechanical staccato.
Ugly short infantry of the mind. . . .

Hemingway's poems may have shown a certain promise, but it quickly became evident that his prose already possessed an exceptional quality of its own. He launched into a series of short stories featuring Nick Adams and other alter egos. These returned to incidents from Hemingway's life, ranging from Michigan to Kansas City to Italy. The stories were linked by a series of vignettes in italic, describing largely violent scenes from the war, America, and Spanish bullfights.

He drew out the sword from the folds of the muleta *and sighted with the same movement and called to the bull, Toro! Toro! And the bull charged and Villalta charged and just for a moment they became one . . . and then it was over. Villalta standing straight and the red hilt of the sword sticking out dully between the bull's shoulders. Villalta, his hand up at the crowd and the bull roaring blood, looking straight at Villalta and his legs caving.*

41

This entire collection was eventually called *In Our Time*. It indicates both Hemingway's intention and his ambitions. His book was intended to show what it meant to be alive in the early twentieth century. This was what life was like, this was how we lived in our modern era. Such may be a large ambition, but *In Our Time* succeeds in its own way in conveying just this.

Hemingway felt that what he had written was new, authentic, and good. He sent the manuscript of *In Our Time* to America, convinced it would soon find a publisher. But it was too new: no one recognized the collection's worth. Eventually Sherwood Anderson put in a good word for Hemingway at his own publishers, where his opinion as their best-selling author carried some weight. As a result, *In Our Time* was accepted by Boni & Liveright. To Hemingway's annoyance, though, the publishers remained cautious, printing just over a thousand copies and spending little on publicity. The book received only a few reviews, some of them favorable. Then a copy passed into the hands of the young and successful Scott Fitzgerald, the much-lauded chronicler of the Jazz Age. Fitzgerald at once spotted the book's genuine qualities and wrote of Hemingway with unstinting admiration. Soon Hemingway's hopes were beginning to be reflected in rising sales figures.

Yet he continued to hold a grudge against Boni & Liveright, and he now began to exhibit an unpleasant trait that would become increasingly evident in his character. He turned on the very people who had helped him. According to the terms of Hemingway's contract, he was obligated to submit his next work to Boni & Liveright. But Hemingway had become convinced that his best hope of fame and fortune lay with the publisher Scribner, whose renowned editor Maxwell Perkins was already launching a number of writers to literary stardom. Typical of these was Thomas Wolfe, who would deliver a vast manuscript that Perkins would cut and slash, reducing the flabby original to a superbly constructed masterpiece. Hemingway's prose was the very opposite: every well-chosen word had its precise place, and no editorial cutting was necessary. Even so, Hemingway was determined to have Perkins as his editor. To effect this, he wrote a vicious parody of Sherwood Anderson called *The Torrents of Spring*. It was naturally rejected by Boni & Liveright, then accepted by Scribner, who was willing to publish this squib as the price for obtaining what they hoped was a major author in the making. The opening lines give a fair idea of the heavy-handed humor to follow:

> Yogi Johnson stood looking out of the window of a big pump-factory in Michigan. Spring would soon be here. Could it be that what this writing fellow Hutchinson had said, "If winter comes can spring be far behind?" would be true again this year? Yogi Johnson wondered.

This was intended as a wicked parody of Anderson's somewhat pedestrian style—which had previously played a formative role in Hemingway's own early style. Hadley was furious at Hemingway's ingratitude to their old friend; Anderson himself maintained a hurt but dignified silence. Astonishingly, Scott Fitzgerald reckoned

The Torrents of Spring to be "about the best comic book ever written by an American." Another person who liked it, and enthusiastically told Hemingway so, was an American woman living in Paris called Pauline Pfeiffer. Pauline was rich and chic, and made no secret of her admiration for Hemingway—both as a writer and as a man. She also fulfilled another Hemingway requirement, being in her early thirties and several years older than he. Hemingway, for his part, found her increasingly sympathetic—to the point where they soon gave up all pretense of concealing their feelings for each other.

Hemingway now had a young son: John, nicknamed "Bumby," for whom he was a surprisingly modern and caring father. He even changed Bumby's diapers on occasion. Even so, the effort of bringing up baby inevitably fell to Hadley. After a long hard day, Hemingway would expect the exhausted Hadley to come out with him in the evenings to the all-night cycle races at the Vélodrome d'Hiver, or for long drinking sessions at the cafés. Hemingway had now met Scott Fitzgerald and had also been introduced to James Joyce. But he also knew a growing number of rich socialite Americans in Paris, hedonistic members of what was becoming known as the "Lost Generation." This was the height of the "Roaring Twenties," the era of the Charleston, flappers, and independent young women with "bobbed" hair, when many well-heeled Americans fled to Europe to escape the rigors of recently introduced Prohibition in America.

Despite such distractions, and frequent holidays for skiing and fishing trips, Hemingway remained a highly focused writer and worked hard. He continued writing a stream of short stories and settled down to his first serious full-length novel. (*The Torrents of Spring* had made just over a hundred sparsely printed pages. According to Hemingway's boast, included in a "Final Note to the Reader," the entire thing "took me ten days to write." This was hardly a novel and was certainly not serious.) His first real novel would take him considerably longer and would be a much more serious undertaking. It would eventually be called *The Sun Also Rises*.

The story of *The Sun Also Rises* is highly revealing of the company that Hemingway was now keeping—charting, as it does, the antics and disillusionment of the Lost Generation in some of the playgrounds of Europe. The story is narrated by Jake Barnes, an American journalist who is sexually impotent after being wounded in the First World War. This wound reflects both Hemingway's earlier fears and his current situation. His considerable guilt over the gradual breakup of his marriage and his deepening involvement with Pauline Pfeiffer may well have rendered him, at least for a short period, literally as well as symbolically impotent. Hemingway the true writer was still in the ascendancy over Hemingway the boaster. The background presence of the blowhard is nonetheless apparent in the opening chapters of the novel, which takes place in Paris. These superbly evoke the inconsequential Parisian nightlife of rich American and British socialites, expatriates, and hangers-on. The dialogue has a superb authenticity, filled with understatement and subtle humor, and intimates the deeper nature of the characters and their relationships. It is as if we are there, listening at the same table, crammed into yet another taxi on the way to yet another club. Yet one can't escape the fact that Jake rather regards himself as the local wise man. He "knows" Paris, in the best travel-guide sense, and makes sure the reader knows this. He knows the tricks of the street traders, which are the latest "in" places to go, and so on:

> The taxi stopped in front of the Rotonde. No matter what café in Montparnasse you ask a taxi-driver to bring you to from the right bank of the river, they always take you to the Rotonde. Ten years from now it will probably be the Dôme. It was near enough, anyway. I walked past the sad tables of the Rotonde to the Select.

Despite this insistent undercurrent of knowingness, Hemingway's clarity of style retains a certain openness. This was intentional. Hemingway knew precisely what he was doing at this stage, and the apparent ease and artlessness of his writing conceals its hidden depths. Although the story appears to recount the escapades of the Lost Generation with some involvement, it soon becomes clear that Hemingway distances himself from these people. Each, in his own way, is a flawed wastrel. In the guise of a compelling narrative, here is an expression of the moral emptiness of such people. In masterly fashion, Hemingway succeeds in maintaining a difficult balance: he both involves the reader and encourages his distaste.

This fascinated disgust very much echoed Hemingway's personal reaction to the Lost Generation. These were the people among whom he spent much of his time: he was capable of enjoying their company but couldn't help feeling repelled by their vacuousness.

The narrative of *The Sun Also Rises* passes from the cafés of Paris to a fishing trip in the mountains of the Basque country. This idyll is superbly evoked:

> I did not feel the first trout strike. When I started to pull up I felt that I had one and

brought him, fighting and bending the rod almost double, out of the boiling water at the foot of the falls, and swung him up onto the dam. He was a good trout, and I banged his head against the timber so that he quivered out straight, and then slipped him into my bag.

Once more Hemingway feels the need to show us that there is a correct way of doing these things, which he of course knows. Here again we see the legacy of the father as well as the fact that we all have to stand in for the younger brother he never had. This insistence on corrections had begun as a literary device in his short stories but was now showing signs of fulfilling a psychological need.

After the peaceful rural joys of the fishing trip, the action passes on to the nonstop clamor and crowds of the fiesta of San Firmin at Pamplona. Here Jake joins up once again with his expatriate friends—including Brett Ashley, the impetuous aristocratic young Englishwoman who is in love with him. Jake also feels deeply for her, but he is aware that his impotence rules out the possibility of any full relationship between them. There is an element of stoic nobility in his acceptance of this situation. Brett in turn spurns the advances of the unpleasant American writer Robert Cohn.

These and other shifting relationships unfold amidst the endless café conversations, the incessant drinking, the running of the bulls, the bullfighting, and even human fighting. The company drifts from bar to bar throughout the night, drinking yet more Fundador (Spanish brandy):

> At the Café Suizo we had just sat down and ordered Fundador when Robert Cohn came up.
>
> "Where's Brett?" he asked.
>
> "I don't know."
>
> "She was with you."
>
> "She must have gone to bed."
>
> "She's not."
>
> "I don't know where she is."
>
> His face was sallow under the light. He was standing up.
>
> "Tell me where she is."

"Sit down," I said. "I don't know where she is."

"The hell you don't!"

"You can shut your face."

And so on, page after page. This, one can't help feeling, is exactly what it must have been like to spend a night among the Lost Generation.

Brett eventually falls for the bullfighter Pedro Romero and runs off with him to Madrid. Eventually she sends a telegram summoning Jake, who learns that she has broken up with Romero, leaving him free to pursue his heroic and noble calling. In the final scene of the novel, Jake and Brett travel through the streets of Madrid in a taxi. Jake puts his arm around Brett, and she exclaims: "We could have had such a damn good time together." "Yes," replies Jake. "Isn't it pretty to think so?"

The essential emptiness and impossibility of their relationship echoes the emptiness and ephemerality of their friends. But their awareness of the hopelessness of their situation suggests that they are not entirely lost despite the company they choose to keep.

The Sun Also Rises has its moments, as well as its longeurs. Indeed, many of the critics even found the later endless conversations both as lively and engaging as the opening ones. The book was published in 1926 to widespread critical acclaim, which quickly translated into good sales. It seemed that people were ready for a book that described empty hedonistic behavior, and the two main characters even served as role models among those who regarded themselves as members of the Lost Generation. "Disillusion" became all the rage among college students. Young women with bobbed hair began to echo Brett's independence and the way she talked ("I was a fool to go away. . . . One's an ass to leave Paris.") The men, on the other hand, saw themselves as the tough, laconic Jake (while choosing to overlook the impotence that prompted him to behave in this fashion).

With *The Sun Also Rises* Hemingway had at last achieved the fame that he felt was his due—the fame that from now on would dog him like a shadow. A year later he published *Men Without Women*, a collection of short stories, many of which featured strong, silent heroes in the Hemingway mold. But these men without women were far from being parody figures. The situations in which they found themselves, and the way they reacted to them, were emblematic of what was to become the Hemingway credo—"grace under pressure." Bereft of consoling or softening female company, these undemonstrative men faced their destiny with heroic fortitude. *Men Without Women* contains some of Hemingway's finest writing, and some of these stories would justly achieve classic status, taking their place among the finest short stories ever written—in English or any language.

Quintessential among these fine, unshowy stories is "The Killers." It tells of two contract killers from Chicago who arrive at a cheap, out-of-town eatery. They have been sent to murder Ole Anderson, an ex-prizefighter living in a nearby rooming house who goes to the eatery each night for his dinner. The denouement of this sparse, seemingly effortless tale succeeds in being chilling, somehow inevitable, even compassionate, and deeply resonant. This apparently artless tale of facing death is but the essential skeleton of a much larger body of experience which we are left pondering after the end of its brief seventeen pages.

Another typical piece is "Fifty Grand," one of the finest boxing stories of all time. It succeeds in the difficult task of showing corruption living alongside honor in a world of deals and double deals. Here we are very much inside the boxing world, which the public sees only from the outside. Hemingway shows us that what the public may suspect is only the half of it. The real thing is both tough and amoral, with money as both the ultimate motive and the ultimate delusion. Yet despite everything, what happens in the ring remains central—to Hemingway, the story, and its combatants. Even here, amidst the fouls, thrown fights, and brutality, there can still be honor—both regardless of what the combatants know, and in a curious way *because* of what they know. They are the corrupt innocents at the heart of the matter—from which the crowd, who do not know the fight is fixed, will always remain excluded:

> Jack climbed up and bent down to go through the ropes and Walcott came over from his corner and pushed the rope down for Jack to go through. The crowd thought that was wonderful. Walcott put his hand on Jack's shoulder and they stood there just for a second.
>
> "So you're going to be one of these popular champions," Jack says to him. "Take your goddam hand off my shoulder."
>
> "Be yourself," Walcott says.
>
> This is all great for the crowd. How gentlemanly the boys are before the fight! How they wish each other luck!

Hemingway skillfully lets us have it both ways. We are right in the midst of the crowd noise, able to hear what the boxers are saying, yet we can also see the event as a spectator. When Hemingway forgot to brag about all he knew, and instead merely let his few well-chosen words convey the scene, his expertise and his vision became one.

Other stories are about Italy, Spain, even bicycle racing. And there are also a couple of duds: one about the Roman soldiers after Christ's crucifixion, and another about a grotesque Austrian incident. These too have their resonances, but for some reason don't quite come off. At this stage of his work, despite his tough-guy subject matter, Hemingway's art was as delicate as a soufflé. The fact that one or two of his soufflés collapsed only serves to emphasize the consummate artistry and confection that went into the making of the ones that succeeded.

After Hemingway and Hadley were divorced, he married Pauline in 1927. The whole business left Hemingway feeling deeply guilty, not an emotion he found it easy to live with. He also became increasingly accident-prone. Some have wondered whether there might perhaps have been a psychological link between the two. Either way, the list of accidents and ailments that now befell Hemingway was of characteristically exaggerated proportions. Some were distinctly unheroic, such as his recurrent attacks of toothache and hemorrhoids. He also began suffering from grippe. His defective eye had kept him out of the army; now, on a visit to his son, Bumby accidentally stuck his finger into the other eye, rendering him all but blind for several days. But this didn't stop Hemingway from going on a skiing holiday—where he suffered no less than ten assorted accidents, crashes, and spills. As if this farcical situation were not bad enough, on his return to Paris he suffered a whopping accident. Returning drunk to his apartment late one night, instead of pulling the lavatory chain he yanked the cord that opened the skylight window, causing the entire skylight to come crashing down on his head. He was left with a large, permanent, and highly visible scar on his forehead. This scar would, over the years, take on the heroic legacy of the 227 shrapnel wounds covered by his trousers. During late-night drinking sessions Hemingway had frequently felt obliged to lower his trousers in order to demonstrate to the assembled company the extent of his war wounds. Now, instead of resorting to this unbalancing self-exposure, he had only to indicate his head to show how close he had come to death. The fact that this wound had been received in the lavatory, rather than in the trenches, was quickly forgotten.

Hemingway was now beginning to tire of exile in Europe. As if his string of accidents were not enough, everywhere he went seemed to remind him of his previous marriage, reawakening his guilt. He felt a growing homesickness for America and in 1928 decided it was time to return. But he had no intention of going back to Chicago; instead he would set up on the island fishing village of Key West in the Gulf of Mexico, at the remote end of the Florida keys. It was the southernmost point of U.S. territory, about as far as one could get from the mainland while remaining in the country. For Hemingway, urban America, ordinary everyday American life, seemed to represent a reality he could no longer face. The suburban world in which he had grown up was too limiting. His literary imagination needed freedom from the quotidian, just as his self-image needed to expand beyond the limits of banal truth. Here in Key West Hemingway could write undisturbed, and during his free time he could fish. Catching trout in small mountain streams was no longer enough; now he could set out into the ocean in a fast motor cruiser and fish for big game—man-sized marlin, barracuda, sharks, and the like. Another deciding factor in his choice of location was undoubtedly the relaxed local interpretation of the Prohibition laws. While mainland America remained dry, apart from speakeasies selling bootleg liquor, Key West's smugglers ensured that the best Cuban rum and Scotch whiskey were readily available for thirsty local fishermen.

Hemingway now settled down to write the book he had been mulling over for years. This was to be set in Italy and would mark his coming to terms with his experiences in war and love. Gone would be the tall stories of the braggart, and in their place the simple telling of truth, in the style that Hemingway had made his own. The book's double-edged title would mark his leave-taking from the arms of his first love and the lethal arms of his first war; he would call it *A Farewell to Arms*.

From the opening passage, *A Farewell to Arms* shows Hemingway at his best:

Troops went by the house and down the road and the dust they raised powdered the leaves of the trees. The trunks of the trees too were dusty and the leaves fell early that year and we saw the troops marching along the road and the dust rising and the leaves, stirred by the breeze, falling and the soldiers marching and afterwards the road bare and white except for the leaves.

A Farewell to Arms is narrated by Frederic Henry, an American volunteer ambulance driver with the Italian army. He meets and falls in love with an English nurse, Catherine Barkley. When Frederic is badly wounded by a mortar and sent to a military hospital in Milan for surgery, Catherine manages to obtain a post at the hospital and nurses him. Their relationship deepens as he recovers through the summer. In a finely realized scene, they go with friends to the San Sciro racetrack. As he is on the point of returning to the trenches, she tells him that she is pregnant, but she refuses to marry him as she doesn't want to be sent home. Frederic returns to the front and takes part in the Italian retreat from Caporetto. This section includes some superb descriptions of what it is like to be part of an army in retreat: "There was no need to confuse our retreat. The size of the army and the fewness of the roads did that. Nobody gave any orders. . . ." He manages to convey the whole as well as the particulars:

> I do not know what I had expected—death perhaps, and shooting in the dark, and running, but nothing happened. We waited, lying flat beyond the ditch along the main road while a German battalion passed. . . . I had not realized how gigantic the retreat was. The whole country was moving, as well as the army. We walked all night, making better time than the vehicles.

Eventually Frederic deserts and rejoins Catherine, but he soon learns that he is due to be arrested. He escapes, together with Catherine, by rowing at night twenty miles up Lake Maggiore into neutral Switzerland. Later, after a difficult childbirth, Catherine dies in a Swiss hospital. At the end, Frederic goes into the hospital room where her body is lying, and asks the nurses to leave:

> But after I had got them out and shut the door and turned off the light it wasn't any good. It was like saying goodbye to a statue. After a while I went out and left the hospital and walked back to the hotel in the rain.

Frederic's relationship with Catherine is artfully counterbalanced by the horrors and destruction of the war that is destroying Europe. *A Farewell to Arms* also managed the difficult feat of appealing to those who wished to read about war as well as those who wished to be moved by the story of a romance. Only very occasionally do ominous telltale signs of the know-all Hemingway intrude—as for instance when Frederic, a mere ambulance driver, corrects one of the Italian soldiers when a shell explodes close to the dugout in which they are sheltering:

> Something landed outside that shook the earth.

"Four hundred twenty or minnenwerfer," Gavuzzi said.

"There aren't any four hundred twenties in the mountains," I said.

"They have big Skoda guns, I've seen the holes."

"Three hundred fives."

Despite the Wall Street crash, which occurred within months of publication, *A Farewell to Arms* continued to sell well; and just three years later it was made into a film starring the young Cary Grant. To Hemingway's disgust, the film-makers gave the movie version a happy ending, with Catherine surviving. As Hemingway was to learn, again and again, in so many ways, popularity had its cost.

The description in *A Farewell to Arms* of Catherine's childbirth and disastrous complications was in fact taken from life. Hemingway's second wife Pauline had been through a similar experience when giving birth to his second son, Patrick, the difference being that she had survived. But another member of the Hemingway family did not survive these years. Prey to ever deepening depressions, one night Hemingway's father shot himself in the head in an upstairs room in the family home at Oak Park. His wife Grace and his thirteen-year-old son Leicester were in the house and heard the shot. It was Leicester who discovered the body, an event from which he never fully recovered. Years later, he too would commit suicide in a similar fashion.

Meanwhile Hemingway continued on his accidental way. He tore his fingers to the bone in a fishing, or boating, accident—the accounts varied even by the time he reached shore. And now Hemingway was beginning to drink heavily. True to character, he had a heroic capacity. Three bottles of red wine with his Spam and pickled onion breakfast were not a rare occurrence. Such meals must have been as punishing for his grippe-racked digestive tract as they were for his liver. Suffering from writer's block, he decided to try bear-hunting in Wyoming. Here he was in the habit of breakfasting on odiferously gamy bearsteaks smeared with marmalade. Such eating habits may appear strange for one who had lived so long in Paris, the capital of haute cuisine, and was also highly appreciative of Italian as well as Spanish cuisine. But apparently Hemingway's breakfast habits were his homegrown tough-guy version of more delicately prepared European dishes—using, in the best self-reliant hunter's fashion, whatever ingredients came to hand.

Then, once again, accident struck—this time in the form of a serious motor accident, when his Ford truck ran off the road and ended upside down in a ditch. How much the local interpretation of the Prohibition laws had to do with this is uncertain, but the result was that Hemingway suffered a multiple fracture of his right arm, the one he used for writing. Mentally unable to write, he had now rendered himself physically unable to do so as well.

Possibly in search of less debilitating distractions, he returned to Europe. Here he decided to travel to Spain to watch the bulls, and occasionally the bullfighters, suffering their own gruesome accidents in the ring. Since his creative abilities remained blocked, he turned instead to reportage. During his tour of the bullrings Hemingway began taking notes for a full-length book about bullfighting, to be called *Death in the Afternoon*. This not only enabled him to use his reporter's descriptive skills and his insider knowledge gained from many years of following this "sport," but also allowed him to continue his meditations on life and death. Perhaps inevitably, the result was a long, rambling, distinctly self-indulgent paean to an esoteric ritual slaughter which it seems only the Spaniards can fully understand. Which is not to say that outsiders remain immune to its mesmerizing effects. Those who have witnessed the spectacle of a bullfight, with its elements dating from ancient, possibly primeval times, often find themselves stirred, in spite of themselves, on some subrational level. When experienced in this manner, it is difficult to judge precisely what is taking place—both within us, and on the gore-spattered sand of the arena. The ritual seems to resonate with a primitive sacrificial urge in our blood. It is somehow both murderous and religious. Hemingway addresses this at the outset:

> I suppose, from a modern moral point of view, the whole bullfight is indefensible; there is certainly much cruelty, there is always danger, either sought or unlooked for, and there is always death, and I should not try to defend it now, only to tell honestly the things I have found true about it.

And this is what he does. Unfortunately, the way in which he chooses to do so is almost a parody. Hemingway's wide-ranging anecdotal manner allows him to indulge in all his worst faults—and this over 350 pages. By the end, instead of knowing all about bullfighting, one cannot help feeling that one has simply been in the presence of a know-all going endlessly on and on about bullfighting. Not for nothing did one American critic of *Death in the Afternoon* head his review "Bull in the Afternoon."

This said, Hemingway's book remains one of the few serious treatments of the subject by a knowledgeable non-Spaniard, and as such is worthy of a measure of respect. Search the book, rather than read it consecutively, and you will find that this respect is at least partly deserved. There are nuggets of fascinating corrida lore, and some fine descriptions of memorable performances as well as disasters. The art of the bullfight is searching in the extreme for the bullfighter. Hemingway offers great insight into such aspects of nobility, bravery, cowardice, recklessness, and failure of nerve as are revealed in bullfighting. In our sophisticated, ironic modern age we find it difficult to treat the more noble elements of human nature directly, in any serious form, and Hemingway's book is a rare instance of a convincing modern attempt to do so. The roots of bullfighting are ancient enough for it to survive our scorn, though for how much longer it is difficult to say. Hemingway's description of the matador's duel with death, uneven though the contest may be, make it a suitable metaphor for certain timeless aspects of the human condition. As Hemingway shows, at some length, it is the *way* the man fights that is judged. Honor at all costs—his famous "grace under pressure"—is what is valued in the contest. As Hemingway puts it when referring to an unfortunate matador of doubtful temperament in a crucial encounter: "It was preferable that he be gored rather than run from the bull." This attitude does not sit easily with our modern compassionate and self-preserving sensibilities. It does no harm to expose oneself to such an attitude, one which was viable—for better or worse—through many centuries before humanity began to enter its liberal democratic era.

Death in the Afternoon often descends into the Hemingway lecturing syndrome, when he can be either patronizing or bullying. On the other hand, there are many fine bullfighting passages which rise above this. His understanding of what is happening in this chthonic ritual has meaning to us far beyond the bullring:

Aside from the normal physical and mental stages the bull goes through in the ring, each individual bull changes his mental state all through the fight. The most common, and to me the most interesting, thing that passes in the bull's brain is the development of querencias.

He goes on to explain this fundamental concept:

> A querencia is a place . . . which develops in the course of the fight where the bull makes his home. It . . . develops in his brain as the fight goes on . . . in his querencia he is dangerous and almost impossible to kill.

The querencia may develop from familiarity, such as the door through which the bull entered the ring. Or it may develop through any number of things, such as where the bull has killed a horse in the earlier stages of the fight with the picador, or where the sand feels cool under his hooves, or where he smells blood from the previous bullfight. As Hemingway explains, any experienced bullfighter knows that the bull will, after a series of passes, be inclined to head back for the querencia he has established, paying no attention to anything in his path. Thus a bullfighter can at this point make a spectacular and seemingly daring pass as the bull goes by. Such passes may appear brilliant, expressing grace, nobility, the very pinnacle of the bullfighter's art, "but to the person who knows bullfighting they are worthless except as tricks." Despite his lapses, Hemingway still knew how to spot the difference between the bull and bull.

In 1933, Hemingway published yet another collection of short stories, entitled *Winner Take Nothing*. The title appears to be taken from an old book on the rules of gambling, which Hemingway quotes in the epigraph to the book:

> Unlike all other forms of lutte or combat the conditions are that the winner shall take nothing; neither his ease, nor his pleasure, nor any notions of glory; nor, if he win far enough, shall there be any reward within himself.

This neatly encapsulates Hemingway's tragiheroic concepetion of combat. Too neatly, perhaps. In fact, this epigraph was made up by Hemingway himself. One unkind critic even went so far as to claim that this was the most convincing bit of creative writing in the entire book. After all the tough-guy antics, the hunt for ever-larger game, and the pretentiousness of *Death in the Afternoon*, the critics had decided to go in for their own form of big-game hunting, and Hemingway was the prey. This was unfair. Although *Winner Take Nothing* is not quite up to the high standard of *Men Without Women*, it remains nontheless a good, if somewhat mixed, collection of stories. A few of them are deeper and darker than his earlier work. The Nick Adams story "A Way You'll Never Be" returns to northern Italy during the First World War and is a subtle evocation of Nick going mad at the front. He dreams of a yellow house, rambles about grasshoppers, and reassures the Italian soldiers he is with that the Americans will soon come to their aid. We are able to see him from within his own mind as well as through the eyes of the wondering and increasingly worried Italians. He tells the Italians how to catch the grasshoppers:

> The correct procedure, and which should be taught all young officers at every small-arms

course if I had anything to say about it, and who knows but what I shall have, is the employment of a seine or net made of common mosquito netting. Two officers holding this length of netting at alternate ends . . .

Despite being at the front, he refuses to wear his helmet:

"You know they're absolutely no damn good," Nick said. "I remember when they were a comfort when we first had them, but I've seen them full of brains too many times."

The Italian officer in charge quietly but firmly insists that Nick leave the front lines. The story is a triumph of understatement. As with so many of his finest stories, Hemingway manages to convey so much more atmosphere, so much more inter-action, and so much more meaning than the spare words of the story offer. A single scene conveys the experience of an entire war.

Another Nick Adams story, "Fathers and Sons," gives a moving, clear-eyed portrait of Hemingway's own father. Other stories are less successful: for instance, "The Mother of a Queen," a thinly disguised expression of Hemingway's feelings for his mother.

At the time, Hemingway was supporting his mother on a monthly allowance; despite being rich and famous, and not an overly mean man, he resented this obligatory charity. In a letter written around this time, he compared his feelings for his mother to shooting game birds: "I would shoot my own mother if she went in coveys and had a good straight flight." Friends spoke of much less subtle, or repeatable, tirades about his mother. Many amateur psychologists, resorting to a fashionable Freudianism, suspected that Hemingway's public tirades of hate for his mother were a cover for rather more Oedipal feelings. His friend the writer John Dos Passos was more perceptive; he reckoned that Hemingway was the only person he had ever met who *really* hated his mother.

By now Hemingway's love of hunting had led him to Africa, to hunt the biggest game of all. He went on safari to Kenya, taking along his wife Pauline. This proved to be a tactical error when husband and wife had a row over who had been the first to shoot a lion. (She had shot it first, but his bullet had then killed it.) Still, he was definitely the first to shoot a rhino and a buffalo and many other lesser species, all of which were duly decapitated to mount as trophies for his game room back home. When he returned to Key West, Hemingway immediately started a book called *Green Hills of Africa*. His aim was "to write an absolutely true book to see whether the shape of a country and the pattern of a month's action can, if truly presented, compete with a work of the imagination." In order to set down his wartime experiences properly, he had waited eight years. But this new work was not to be a work of the imagination, it was to be an "absolutely true autobiography." His continuing insistence on this score inevitably incurs suspicion. Indeed, his repeated insistence on the phrase "absolutely true" appears too good to be true. And of course it is. When he came to write this book, Hemingway found himself in a difficult situation. Pauline's wealthy Uncle Gus, the owner of a prominent pharmaceutical company, had paid for the Hemingways' trip to Kenya. (Big-game hunting was a preserve of the super-rich; Hemingway was still merely a well-off writer.) All this meant that there was little room in Hemingway's book for true accounts of violent marital rows over lion priority. The incident in question was merely elided into some amiable joshing with Pauline, who is referred to as P.O.M. (Poor Old Mama) throughout the book.

> "You know, I feel as though I did shoot it," P.O.M. said. "I don't believe I'd be able to stand it if I really had shot it. I'd be too proud. Isn't triumph marvelous? . . ."
>
> "I believe you did shoot him," I said.
>
> "Oh, let's not go into that," P.O.M. said. "I feel so wonderful about just being supposed to have killed him. . . ."
>
> "Good old Mama," I said. "You killed him."
>
> "No, I didn't. Don't lie to me. Just let me enjoy my triumph."

Grace under pressure was one thing, but grace in defeat was not a Hemingway trait—except in fiction. But this was only part of Hemingway's difficulties in writing *Green Hills of Africa*. Not long after beginning the book, Hemingway temporarily moved to Havana, a hundred miles or so across the water from Key West, leaving Pauline behind. In Havana he had an affair with a fun-loving strawberry blonde named Jane Mason, the twenty-five-year-old wife of an expatriate American airline executive. In part through guilt, and in part because he reckoned he owed it to Uncle Gus, Hemingway now began attesting in his "absolutely true autiobiography" how much his wife had meant to him on their safari together: "The only person I really cared about, except the children, was with me and I had no wish to share this life with anyone who was not there."

Quite apart from these papered-over flaws, *Green Hills of Africa*, published in 1935, is the first book to mark a genuine decline in Hemingway's writing. (Sufficiently cut, *Death in the Afternoon* could well have been the discerning *jeu d'esprit* of an aficionado.) Still, he retained elements of his old writing self; the truth seeps up from beneath the surface, despite the author's failing powers. At one point he discusses with a fellow hunter how America destroys its writers:

> First, economically. They make money. . . . Then our writers when they have made some money increase their standard of living and they are caught. They have to write to keep up their establishments, their wives, and so on, and they write slop. It is slop not on purpose but because it is hurried.

Hemingway would claim that such sentiments were provoked by the fate of his friends John Dos Passos and Scott Fitzgerald (who perceptively noted, "There are no second acts in American lives"). Dos Passos was reduced to writing for Hollywood, and Fitzgerald was churning out stories about high society for the magazines—both well into the "second act" of their careers. This was the stage that Hemingway too was now entering as a writer (as a man he was already well into some nonexistent third act of his own imagining).

Hemingway would eventually salvage something from his big-game hunting experiences, but this would take time and brooding. Some years later he used this African setting for two of his more ambitious short stories, "The Snows of Kilimanjaro" and "The Short Happy Life of Francis Macomber." "Snows" indicates the depth of his worries about what was happening to him. He knew he was destroying himself, yet he felt that the writer should attempt to transform such material into art. The epigraph of this story hints at his attempt.

> *Kilimanjaro is a snow covered mountain 19,710 feet high, and is said to be the highest mountain in Africa. Its western summit is called the Masai 'Ngàje Ngài, the House of God. Close to the western summit there is the dried and frozen carcass of a leopard. No one has explained what the leopard was seeking at that altitude.*

Hemingway had by now convinced himself that a man could be possessed of heroism only if he constantly put it to the test. This notion evolved into a hunt for ever more exciting game. He had fished off Key West and off Havana, but

80

then he learned that the best fishing in the region was to be had at Bimini Island, in the Bahamas. To get there he needed a boat of his own. So he bought a thirty-eight-foot diesel-powered cruiser, which he named *Pilar* (the secret nickname he had used for Pauline when they first fell in love). This set him back $7,500 in all, a huge sum in those depression days, and its name suggests that some of the money for this big boy's toy may have come from his rich wife. On his first trip to Bimini, some 180 miles northeast of Key West, he took along Dos Passos and his wife Katy. For some reason Pauline was left behind. The trip quickly became a disaster. Twenty miles out of port, Hemingway caught a large shark. Having reeled it in, he decided the best way to kill it was with his .22 caliber automatic pistol. Somehow he succeeded in shooting not only the shark but also himself, in *both* legs, and spraying his new boat with ricocheting bullets. The hired helmsman refused to go farther and immediately headed back for Key West while Katy Dos Passos angrily berated the slumped hero for all but shooting everyone on board.

In early September 1935 the Florida Keys were hit by the so-called Great Hurricane, the worst to strike the region in years. The main force of the hurricane missed Key West, and the *Pilar* managed to ride out the storm in the protection of the local submarine base. But the northern islands in the keys, such as Key Largo and the Matecumbe Keys, were all but swept clean, with a large loss of life. When Hemingway sailed north, he was horrified by the devastation he saw. On Lower Matecumbe Key he saw the remains of the two women who had run the local gas station, "naked, tossed up into the trees by the water, swollen and stinking, their breasts as big as balloons, flies between their legs." A thousand unemployed war veterans working on a New Deal project were killed overnight. The vets had been crammed into ramshackle camps, and their government employers had simply left them to die in the storm, without proper warning or protection. The disaster prompted Hemingway to write an angry, hard-hitting article entitled "Who Killed the Vets?" He castigated "wealthy people, yachtsmen, fishermen such as

President Hoover and President Roosevelt," who simply sailed off north in their boats at the beginning of the hurricane season. They were interested only in saving their property. "But veterans . . . are not property. They are only human beings, unsuccessful human beings, and all they have to lose is their lives."

Hemingway now found himself embroiled in politics, a subject he had always done his best to avoid. Many left-wing intellectuals had urged Hemingway to speak out about American injustice, and commit himself publicly to the cause of the hard-luck characters he so often described in his work. Hemingway's answer was *To Have and Have Not* (1937), the only novel he was to set in America.

The title led many to expect a full-blown political novel, but Hemingway was incapable of producing such a thing. On the one hand, he was too much of an artist; on the other, he remained mistrustful of any party political line. Never the team player, he was always the individual. The hero of *To Have and Have Not* is Harry Morgan, a tough-guy loner who had already appeared in a couple of Hemingway's short stories. It is now almost impossible to separate the character of Morgan in Hemingway's story from the stylized, hard-bitten character portrayed by Humphrey Bogart in the adventure film made of this work. Sadly, this is neither accidental nor unjust. Harry Morgan is little more than a stereotype; indeed, his portrayal in the film even fleshes him out somewhat, giving him an element of idiosyncratic life that is often missing from the book.

Hemingway had refused to demean himself by working for Hollywood, scorning his friends Dos Passos and Fitzgerald who found themselves forced to such measures during difficult economic times. Even William Faulkner, the only other contemporary American writer whose talent equalled Hemingway's at his best, would end up writing briefly for Hollywood— ironically, working on the script of *To Have and Have Not*. The even greater irony was that Hemingway's books were proving ideal for Hollywood: the film versions of his works would from now on become as memorable as the works themselves.

To Have and Have Not describes Harry Morgan's adventures with his boat in Key West, Cuba, and the waters in between. His unscrupulousness, the tricks played on him by fate, and his sad end proved enough to send Hemingway's book to fourth on the best-seller list. But the critics were bitterly disappointed: there had been high literary hopes for Hemingway. His political supporters were also disappointed. Harry Morgan may have been at the bottom of the social heap, and may have suffered from injustice, but he was hardly a political hero. In fact he was almost devoid of political awareness, except of the most rudimentary kind. "A man alone ain't got no bloody chance," is his creed, a realization he comes to in his dying words. Morgan saw his condition in individual human terms, his fate likewise. Neither Morgan nor Hemingway was capable of collectivization.

Despite this fatal drawback in a political sense, Hemingway persisted with political involvement. In 1936 the Spanish Civil War broke out when the fascist General Franco led the army in an uprising that attempted to overthrow the elected left-wing government. Hemingway received several lucrative offers to cover the war as a correspondent but was not initially tempted. One afternoon, as he was drinking at his favorite Key West watering hole Sloppy Joe's, he met a tawny blonde, tough-talking young journalist named Martha Gellhorn. He was immediately smitten, and when she expressed her desire to go to Spain and cover the war, he characteristically decided he would get there first. Pauline tried everthing she could to keep him home, even going so far as to dye her hair tawny blonde. (During the Jane Mason episode, she had briefly resorted to strawberry blonde.) But all to no avail, and Hemingway set off. While he was away, Pauline did her best to lure him back, building a swimming pool on the grounds of their Key West residence, which had been a late wedding present from Uncle Gus. (Digging this pool proved to be a hugely expensive operation: Key West is an island of solid coral rock—inches beneath the surface, everything had to be pick-axed by teams of laborers.)

By March 1937, Hemingway was installed in an apartment in the swish Hotel Florida in Madrid, along with Martha Gellhorn. He had assured her press agency, the North American Newspaper Alliance, that he would not take sides, but he soon became involved in the anti-fascist cause, undertaking all manner of propaganda ventures and becoming closely involved with their forces. He was in Madrid as Franco's forces bombarded the city in one of the final engagements of the war before the fascist takeover. By now Hemingway's reports had become increasingly personalized, the action mainly centering on the often fictionalized subjective impressions of the intrepid correspondent. The agency sent urgent wires demanding to know what was actually going on in the war, but these were ignored.

Eventually Hemingway returned home to Key West. His guilt spilled over into anger at Pauline over the unwonted and unwanted swimming pool. He then settled down to write his novel of the Spanish Civil War, *For Whom the Bell Tolls*. But halfway through, he decided he could no longer handle the situation at home, and he sailed for Cuba in the *Pilar*, where he set up home in Havana with Martha Gellhorn.

Opinion remains divided on *For Whom the Bell Tolls*. Some critics call it his finest work; it was certainly his most ambitious. In moments of expansiveness, he would declare it to be his attempt at a twentieth-century *War and Peace*. Its themes—love and war—certainly echo those of Tolstoy, but it has none of the social sweep of the Russian work. On the other hand, Hemingway's novel had undoubted ambitions to universality. This is evident from the title, which is based upon words from a funeral sermon by the seventeenth-century English metaphysical poet John Donne:

> . . . any mans *death* diminishes *me*, because I am involved in *Mankinde*; And therefore never send to know for whom the *bell* tolls; It tolls for *thee*.

Hemingway wanted to show that the battle against fascism being fought in the Spanish Civil War affected the entire world. The loss of democratic freedom in Spain would be a blow to freedom everywhere. This was a prescient vision, hardly popular in the isolationist America of the period. By the time Hemingway published this work in 1940, Franco and fascism had triumphed in Spain and Europe was plunged into the Second World War.

The action of *For Whom the Bell Tolls* is based on a true incident that took place during the Spanish Civil War. In Hemingway's version, the American volunteer Robert Jordan joins up with a group of guerrilla fighters operating behind fascist lines in the Guadarrama Mountains north of Madrid. Here he meets and falls in love with Maria. Hemingway explores the cruelties of war and its often meaningless bravery. The latter is exemplified by Jordan's futile mission to blow up a bridge near Segovia.

For Whom the Bell Tolls would prove to be by far and away Hemingway's most popular work, and by 1943 it had sold over three-quarters of a million copies, the biggest best-seller in America since *Gone with the Wind*. As Hemingway wrote in a letter: "Book selling like frozen Daiquiris in hell." Again, the literary critics carped: Hemingway had "souped up" the Civil War, turning it into an essentially popular novel. This was both true and unfair. Hemingway's technique and his treatment of violent subject matter had now been copied by many second-rate popular writers of adventure fiction. It was thus hardly surprising that Hemingway's novels appeared to be descending into this genre. He had done much to invent it in its modern form. Yet the critics had some justification. Hemingway's work had originally been new, its clarity almost experimental in its astonishing freshness. Stylistically he was now repeating himself, resorting to tricks of technique that now appeared well worn. So much so that it was easy to filet out the story line from the book and turn it into another adventure movie—it appeared in 1943, starring Gary Cooper and Ingrid Bergman.

Having completed his book on the pointlessness of war, Hemingway now returned to the battlefield. After marrying Martha Gellhorn, he set off with her on their honeymoon to China, to cover the Sino-Japanese war. Martha's independent manner, which had first so attracted Hemingway, now turned out to be a source of irritation. She turned out to be a genuinely tough war correspondent in her own right, and soon decided that she didn't want Hemingway tagging along and pinching her stories. They ended up covering the war together, but separately. Then they returned to Cuba.

By now it was clear that age wasn't the only big difference between Gellhorn and Hemingway. Habitually dressed in a pair of baggy old shorts and a sweat-stained shirt, Hemingway returned to his fishing and his drinking. Unfortunately he frequently wore the same shirt and shorts for both activities, either of which could continue for days. Despite Martha being used to rough living as a war correspondent, she soon found her pungent husband difficult to take. As she later put it: "I am really not abnormally clean. . . . But Ernest was extremely dirty, one of the most unfastidious men I've ever known." By now America had joined the Second World War, so the two of them got contracts as war correspondents. They set off for Europe, where beleagured Britain was still holding out against the Nazis. It soon became clear that this was not to be a joint reporting mission, and after a series of sharp disagreements the two correspondents began covering the war in their own ways, in separate sectors.

Hemingway holed up in an expensive suite at the Dorchester in London, where he regaled fellow war correspondents over ham and eggs and the best Scotch whiskey for breakfast. Inevitably, the drunken accidents continued. On the way back from a party at 3 a.m. he was involved in a serious car crash, as a result of which he required fifty-seven stitches. He did his best to disguise his latest war wounds from the military authorities, as he needed their permission to join the troops and do his reporting. Unaccountably, he received it, and a somewhat groggy Hemingway set out on a series of increasingly daring missions. He flew on a number of bomber flights, then traveled on an assault craft with some of the first soldiers in the D-day landings. Later he joined up with the advancing American forces. By now he was as incapable of discipline as he was of sobriety. Contrary to all the rules governing the behavior of war correspondents, he formed his own unofficial armed guerrilla group. The other correspondents, whose status with the enemy was thereby compromised, were not amused. Neither were many of the soldiers, bound by discipline and facing death, pleased to see him apparently using the war as his own private adventure. Regardless, Hemingway and his group rushed into Paris with the liberating forces. Here he famously liberated the Ritz, then spent several days liberating the bar of its contents. In the course of these raucous sessions, where he held court to all and sundry, he was rejoined by a fellow American journalist he had met in London. Her name was Mary Welsh, and she soon proved to be more pliant and agreeable than the hard-bitten Mrs. Hemingway the third, who remained busy reporting from the frontline. After a further series of drunken heroics and "subjective reports" from the battlefront, the war in Europe finally ended and Hemingway retired to the Ritz to sleep things off while Martha sued for divorce. A year later, Mary Welsh became the fourth Mrs. Hemingway.

By now almost permanently befuddled, Hemingway launched into another novel. Together with Mary he spent an extended period in Venice conducting research for this work, *Across the River and into the Trees*. The title is taken from the great Civil War General Stonewall Jackson. After being fatally wounded at Chancellorsville in 1863, Jackson's dying words were: "Let us cross over the river and sit under the shade of the trees." Hemingway's novel is also about an old soldier who knows he is about to die. Colonel Richard Cantwell is living in Venice and falls in love with a beautiful young Italian contessa. *Across the River and into the Trees* is a sad, rambling tale written by a ghost of the writer Hemingway had once been. When it was published in 1950 it was generally recognized that Hemingway was finished as a writer. The boastful and bloated "Papa," as his public persona became known by his gang of hangers-on, had now completely taken over the lean, clear-eyed artist.

Or so it seemed. Hemingway remained a tough fighter to the end. Despite returning with

Mary to live in Cuba, where he downed Daiquiris at a rate that would have poleaxed any lesser man, he continued writing. Miraculously, his next book was all that his previous novel had not been. *The Old Man and the Sea* is a tale of mythic resonance, told with classic simplicity. It has the clarity of a parable, yet its epic qualities reach far into the realms of heroic human endeavor. Not a word too many, not a word too few, each sentence has its ringing meaning. Here Hemingway lived up to the dictum of Joseph Conrad, the writer of the previous generation whom he most admired: "A work that aspires, however humbly, to the condition of art should carry its justification in every line." Such is evident in *The Old Man and the Sea* from its opening lines:

> He was an old man who fished alone in a skiff in the Gulf Stream and he had gone eighty-four days now without taking a fish. In the first forty days a boy had been with him. But after forty days without a fish the boy's parents had told him that the old man

was now definitely and finally *salao*, which is the worst form of unlucky. . . .

Amidst this objectivity there is also a poignant subjective self-knowledge. This most objective of Hemingway's stories is also in certain ways his most personal, though not in any autobiographical sense. The tale contains a hard-earned spiritual understanding.

> He knew he was beaten now finally and without remedy and he went back to the stern and found the jagged end of the tiller would fit in the slot of the rudder well enough for him to steer. He settled the sack around his shoulder and put the skiff on her course.

We are instructed in how the old man fishes, and the ways of the Gulf Stream, but we never feel that we are being lectured. We are alongside the old man in his simple yet titanic struggle with fate. This is not a tale of despair: evident defeat leads to a greater victory.

In 1954, Hemingway and Mary went to Africa to hunt big game. This time Hemingway's saga of accidents reached its apotheosis. While flying across the Murchison Falls on the way to the Belgian Congo, the light aircraft in which he was traveling hit an abandoned telegraph wire stretching across the gorge, and the plane crashed into remote jungle. Hemingway had a sprained shoulder, but Mary was badly shocked. It took some time for them to be rescued, and they were lucky to be found at all. A British airliner had eventually spotted the wreckage but had reported that there were no survivors. On his return, Hemingway learned that news of his death had been wired around the world. The *Herald Tribune* in New York was just one of several papers that printed his obituary. Another light aircraft was hired to take Hemingway and Mary to Entebbe in Uganda. Incredibly, this plane crashed on takeoff and burst into flames. Hemingway butted the door open with his head, and Mary followed. Hemingway lay on the ground in a daze, dispiritedly listening to his bottles of booze exploding in the wreckage: "There were four small pops representing the explosion of the bottles of Carlsberg beer which had constituted our reserve . . . followed by a slightly louder pop. . . . After this, I clearly heard a louder but still not intense explosion which I knew signified the unopened bottle of Gordon's gin." And so on.

Later that year Hemingway was awarded the Nobel Prize for Literature. *The Old Man and the Sea*, a tale at least in part about the illusoriness of reputation, had ironically resurrected Hemingway's own reputation. He sent word to the Nobel committee that he would be unable to attend the award ceremony in Stockholm because he was still recovering from his air crashes. This was only partly true. The accidents had done more damage to him than was at first apparent, but his alchoholism was now leading to serious physical and mental deterioration. His final years were a sorry parody. The battered, staggering "Papa" traveled around his old watering holes, much interviewed and much photographed wherever he went. There was a final disastrous trip to Spain and the abandoned manuscript of another bullfighting book. His mind had begun to wander, and he was becoming increasingly paranoid, imagining himself followed everywhere by the FBI. It was plain to all but his most sycophantic fans that he could no longer write.

But once again they were wrong. Over the years, Hemingway had begun setting down memories of his early years in Paris, which he now began assembling into a book. He called it *A Moveable Feast*, though it would only appear posthumously. This book is as lucid and evocative as some of his better work. Even so, it makes for mixed reading. There is the usual boasting, and the settling of a few old scores (most notably with Scott Fitzgerald). Often the tales of derring-do are unintentionally hilarious (such as the trip where he earnestly attempts to cure Fitzgerald of his alcoholism while consuming vast amounts himself). But at the heart of these memoirs is a fine description of what it must have been like to live and work in Paris during those golden years in the twenties:

It was a pleasant café, warm and clean and friendly, and I hung up my old waterproof on the coat rack to dry and put my worn and weathered felt hat on the rack above the bench and ordered a café au lait. The waiter brought it and I took out my notebook from the pocket of the coat and a pencil and started to write.

In 1961, by now a sick and debilitated wreck of his former self, Hemingway returned to the wilds of Ketchum, Idaho. Here he succumbed to the Hemingway family curse and shot himself on July 2, just days before his sixty-second birthday. The Hemingway curse would continue to claim victims after his death, with his younger brother Leicester shooting himself in 1982 and his first granddaughter, the model and actress Margaux Hemingway, taking her life in Hollywood in 1996.

Afterword

Hemingway's reputation has not weathered well. After his death came the social revolution of the sixties, and with it women's liberation. Men were expected to be something more than heroes, constantly testing their valor. Likewise, the public view of hunting underwent a transformation. What had once appeared as a noble sport was now looked upon as the indiscriminate slaughter of innocent beasts. Such attitudes tend to concentrate upon Hemingway and his belligerent persona. The image is bolstered by much of his work, in which the braggart and the tough guy often feature. But such critical myopia overlooks his finest work. The prose of

Hemingway's early stories, and in parts of some of his novels, appears almost as fresh today as it did when it first appeared. It is often forgotten that Hemingway was initally regarded as a revolutionary stylist of the early twentieth century, his work placed alongside early Joyce, the experimentalism of Gertrude Stein, and the formal innovations of John Dos Passos. The latter two have not weathered the passage of time so well, whereas Joyce went on to ever greater achievements. Hemingway, on the other hand, remains deserving of this early high assessment. He was very much a member of that early twentieth-century generation that brought American literature to maturity.

Before this generation America had undeniably produced great writers, but largely in isolation. Herman Melville, Mark Twain, and Henry James immediately spring to mind. But their reputation *as Americans* remained remarkably similar to the world's assessment of the United States as a country: Americans were indeed capable of greatness but seemed to have little tradition of their own, historically or culturally.

This may have been a harsh judgment, based largely upon ignorance, but it undeniably prevailed. All this was to change as America gradually emerged to take its preeminent place on the world's stage. By the mid-twentieth century—a century that was already becoming known as the "American century"—there could be no doubting that America had a firmly established literary tradition. Hemingway was very much a part of this and made his own distinctive contribution to it. The Hemingway character, as established in his finest short stories, seemed to embody something quintessentially American. Such characteristic national identity had not until then been fully established—at least in the eyes of the world. Such an identity was also discernible in the writings of Scott Fitzgerald, whose works did so much to describe the "American dream." At the same time William Faulkner was describing a deeply rooted historical America that had remained overlooked.

With these three great writers, more than any others, America seemed to come of age—historically, culturally, and as a place possessed of a distinctive nationality. To dismiss Hemingway from this formative triumvirate, as many critics seem inclined to do, is to overlook an essential element in the historical self-consciousness of emergent America. Hemingway's conception of "grace under pressure" demands now, perhaps more than for a long time, reinstatement in the American psyche.

Hemingway's Chief Works

Three Stories and Ten Poems (1923)[†]
In Our Time (1925)[*†]
The Torrents of Spring (1926)[†]
The Sun Also Rises (or *Fiesta*) (1926)[*†]
Men Without Women (1927)[*†]
A Farewell to Arms (1929)[*†]
Death in the Afternoon (1932)[†]
Winner Take Nothing (1933)[*†]
Green Hills of Africa (1935)[†]
To Have and Have Not (1937)[†]
For Whom the Bell Tolls (1940)[†]

[*]major works
[†]discussed in text

Across the River and into the Trees (1950)[†]
The Old Man and the Sea (1952)*[†]
A Moveable Feast (1964)[†]

Chronology of Hemingway's Life and Times

1899   Ernest Hemingway born on July 21 at Oak Park, a suburb of Chicago.

1900   Hawaiian Islands become United States territory. Boxer Rebellion against foreign influence in China.

1914   Outbreak of First World War. Woodrow Wilson keeps America out of war with "peace at any price" policy. Opening of Panama Canal.

1917   America joins Allies in First World War. Hemingway becomes reporter with *Kansas City Star.* Bolshevik Revolution in Russia brings Lenin to power.

1918   Spring: Hemingway volunteers for army
        service but is turned down due to
        defective eyesight. Summer: Hemingway
        volunteers for Red Cross service and
        becomes an ambulance driver in
        northern Italy. Hemingway wounded
        and decorated for bravery. November:
        end of First World War. Woodrow
        Wilson attends Versailles Peace
        Conference.

1919   Hemingway returns to America.
        Prohibition law passed.

1920   Hemingway finds work on *Toronto Star*.
        Marries Elizabeth Hadley Richardson and
        moves to Paris.

1922   Mussolini and fascists come to power in
        Italy.

1923   Hemingway's first son, "Bumby," born.
        Three Stories and Ten Poems published in
        Paris.

1925   Hemingway's collection of short stories,
        In Our Time, published in New York.

1926   Gene Tunney defeats Jack Dempsey to
        become world heavyweight boxing

champion. Hemingway publishes satirical
novel, *The Torrents of Spring*. His novel
The Sun Also Rises published, quickly
achieving critical and popular success.

1927   Hemingway publishes short-story
collection *Men Without Women*. Divorced
from Hadley.

1928   Hemingway marries second wife, Pauline
Pfeiffer. Moves to Key West, Florida.
Pauline gives birth with difficulty to
Hemingway's second son, Patrick.
Hemingway's father commits suicide.

1929   Publication of Hemingway's novel about
the First World War, *A Farewell to Arms*.
Wall Street Crash signals worldwide Great
Depression.

1932   Hemingway publishes his book about
bullfighting, *Death in the Afternoon*.

1933   Franklin D. Roosevelt inaugurates New
Deal. Hitler and Nazis take power in
Germany. End of Prohibition in America.

1935   *Green Hills of Africa* published.

1936   Outbreak of Spanish Civil War.

1939   End of Spanish Civil War; Franco and
        fascists take over in Spain. Outbreak of
        Second World War in Europe.

1941   Japanese attack Pearl Harbor. America
        joins Allies in Second World War.
        Hemingway marries third wife, Martha
        Gellhorn.

1942   Hemingway and Martha travel to Far
        East to cover the war in China.

1944   Hemingway and Martha travel to Europe
        to cover the war.

1945   End of Second World War. Hemingway
        divorced from Martha.

1946   Hemingway marries fourth wife, Mary
        Welsh.

1950   Publishes *Across the River and into the
        Trees*, which is savaged by critics.

1952   Triumphantly returns to form with *The
        Old Man and the Sea*.

1954   Hemingway involved in two plane crashes
        in Africa. Awarded Nobel Prize for
        Literature.

1961   Hemingway commits suicide at Ketchum,
        Idaho.

Recommended Reading

Kenneth S. Lynn, *Hemingway* (Simon & Schuster, 1987). This was the famous debunking biography of Hemingway that caused a sensation on its first appearance. It meticulously examines each of Hemingway's exaggerations and boasts, exposing many of them as myths. But its relentlessly negative tone can be a bit much. There was more to Hemingway than the increasingly flawed public figure who eventually took his own life.

Carlos Baker, *Ernest Hemingway* (Penguin, 1969). This exhaustive nine-hundred-page biography is still regarded by many as the standard life, despite its many faults and its tendency to give Hemingway the benefit of the doubt about some of his fibs. This too succeeds in puncturing many of the more blatant myths, but it also succeeds in

bringing the man himself to life: marriages, booz-
ing, hunting, and all—even the writing.

Anthony Burgess, *Ernest Hemingway and His World*
(Thames and Hudson, 1968). This is a sympathetic and perceptive portrait by a fellow writer.
The rather brief text is accompanied by more
than a hundred illustrations. These, as well as any
words, illustrate the man in his high days and in
his decline. The photos of the wars, the hunting,
the café tables, even the book covers tell their
tale. Burgess brings a refreshing European eye to
this most American of Americans who chose to
spend so much of his time in Europe.

Wirt Williams, *The Tragic Art of Ernest Hemingway*
(Louisiana State University Press, 1981). An in-
sightful and sympathetic critical view of Hemingway's works. Provides an interesting view of
Hemingway as a tragedian. In the words of the
great man himself: "All stories, if continued far
enough, end in death, and he is no true story-
teller who would keep that from you."

Frank Scafella, ed., *Hemingway: Essays of Reassess-
ment* (Oxford University Press, 1991). These
highly varied essays contain all manner of in-
triguing investigations into Hemingway's life and
works. There's also a section of half a dozen es-

says on what made the old man tick, by a number of more or less worried psychologists.

Carlos Baker, ed., *Selected Letters of Ernest Hemingway, 1917–1961* (Panther, 1985). Hemingway's personal dispatches to his loved ones, and a few to his not so loved ones—including generals, writers, wives, and even his comments on drinking champagne with Marlene Dietrich while she watches him shaving. From the porcine to the preposterous, but always entertaining and occasionally as movingly bighearted as he thought himself to be.

William White, ed., *By-line: Ernest Hemingway—Selected Articles and Dispatches* (Collins, 1968). Here you can read Hemingway's dispatches from the wars he covered, including his celebrated "How We Came to Paris." Also contains articles on big game hunting in Africa, the Spanish Civil War, marlin fishing off Cuba, and much other high testosterone stuff. Contains some of the best of Hemingway.

Michael S. Reynolds, *The Young Hemingway* (Blackwell, 1986). This work sketches how Hemingway became a writer, identifying many of the formative influences, as well as an interesting look at his early life and times. As you'd expect, nothing less than exciting stuff.

Index

A NOTE ON THE AUTHOR

Paul Strathern has lectured in philosophy and mathematics and now lives and writes in London. He is the author of the enormously successful series Philosophers in 90 Minutes. A Somerset Maugham Prize winner, he is also the author of books on history and travel, as well as five novels. His articles have appeared in a great many publications, including the *Observer* (London) and the *Irish Times*.

Paul Strathern's 90 Minutes series in philosophy, also published by Ivan R. Dee, includes individual books on Thomas Aquinas, Aristotle, St. Augustine, Berkeley, Confucius, Derrida, Descartes, Dewey, Foucault, Hegel, Heidegger, Hume, Kant, Kierkegaard, Leibniz, Locke, Machiavelli, Mars, J. S. Mill, Nietzsche, Plato, Rousseau, Bertrand Russell, Sartre, Schopenhauer, Socrates, Spinoza, and Wittgenstein.